SHROPSHIRE AIRFIELDS

THROUGH TIME

Alec Brew

AMBERLEY

First published 2019

Amberley Publishing
The Hill, Stroud
Gloucestershire, GL5 4EP

www.amberley-books.com

Copyright © Alec Brew, 2019

The right of Alec Brew to be identified as
the Author of this work has been asserted in
accordance with the Copyrights, Designs and
Patents Act 1988.

ISBN 978 1 4456 9629 4 (print)
ISBN 978 1 4456 9630 0 (ebook)

British Library Cataloguing in Publication Data.
A catalogue record for this book is available from
the British Library.

Typeset in 10pt on 13pt Celeste.
Typesetting by Aura Technology and Software
Services, India. Printed in the UK.

Introduction

All across Shropshire silent sightless sentinels watch over fields of grass and wheat. Slowly decaying, windowless control towers, or watch offices as they were once known, are left as proud reminders that the county used to be covered with airfields, training the aircrew who fought the Second World War, not just RAF, but also Fleet Air Arm and American. Clustered across the Shropshire plain, their circuits almost touching, twenty airfields were operating in 1945, which are now mostly gone, returned to agriculture.

Flying came to Shropshire before the First World War, but the itinerant pilots of the day used the nearest handy large grass field – there were no designated airfields. In the First World War, Royal Flying Corps training fields were built at Tern Hill and Shawbury, and a large Aircraft Acceptance Park was built at Monkmoor, adjacent to Shrewsbury, where new aircraft could be delivered by road and then erected and prepared for service. Monkmoor also housed the School of Photography and Aerial Reconnaissance.

After the war all three airfields closed, though Monkmoor was a popular venue for joy-riding companies until the expansion of Shrewsbury engulfed the flying field. The only permanent airfield in the county after that was the gliding field on the top of the Long Mynd, to where the Midland Gliding Club had migrated, from a field at Handsworth, Birmingham, where it had been formed. The Mynd offered steady west winds that aided sustained flight without the need for thermals.

With war looming during the late 1930s, and with the rapid expansion of the Royal Air Force, Shropshire was again seen as an ideal place to build flying training airfields, Aircraft Storage Units (ASUs) and Maintenance Units (MUs) where aircraft could be stored and prepared for service, far from the reach of the Luftwaffe. Shawbury and Tern Hill were naturally chosen once again, but were doubled in size. On the eastern side of the county a new School of Technical Training was built in the fields to the north of Albrighton and called RAF Cosford, with No. 9 MU attached. Monkmoor had lost its airfield to housing but the hangars were returned to use for No. 30 MU, salvaging crashed aircraft.

At High Ercall the biggest airfield in the county was created to house No. 29 MU but also operational fighter squadrons defending the north-west. A dedicated fighter station was built at Atcham, with a Satellite Landing Ground (SLG) at Condover, but in the end RAF Atcham was turned over to the United States Eighth Air Force to train their new fighter pilots in British conditions, and Condover became a satellite for Shawbury. As the war progressed two bomber Operational Training Units (OTUs) were housed, No. 81 OTU's Whitleys at RAF Tilstock, with a satellite airfield at Sleap, and No. 83 OTU's Wellingtons at Child's Ercall, later renamed RAF Peplow.

As bomber crews were trained in the north of Shropshire, over in the west, No. 61 OTU opened at Rednal, training fighter pilots on Spitfires, with a satellite airfield at Montford Bridge. Then in 1942 the Fleet Air Arm were looking for a central airfield to establish a Blind Flying School. RAF Hinstock, originally named Ollerton, had been built as a satellite of RAF Shawbury and was turned over to the Navy, becoming HMS Godwit, one of His Majesty's Ships about as far from the sea as it's possible to be (about 60 miles as a godwit flies). Hinstock also used a satellite airfield at Bratton, just north of Wellington.

With intense flight training across Shropshire, other satellite airfields were established at Bridleway Gate for the use of the Airspeed Oxfords from Shawbury, and at Chetwynd for the Miles Masters of Tern Hill. When the MUs required additional space to store aircraft, Relief Landing Grounds (RLGs) were created at Weston Park, Hodnet and Brockton near Sutton Maddock, incorporating a field where the first ever aircraft had landed in the county – a Deperdussin monoplane, piloted by James Valentine back in 1911.

With Shropshire's skies full of aircraft, Spitfire and Thunderbolt fighters, Wellington and Whitley bombers, Oxford and Master trainers, and any number of other types being ferried to and from the MUs, it was another RAF base that left the greatest impression on so many RAF men and women. Vast numbers of RAF recruits had their initial training at RAF Bridgnorth, which opened in 1939 at Stanmore as No. 4 Recruit Centre. This was never an airfield, but it did leave an indelible impression on all the raw civilians who were knocked into military shape in just six weeks.

Many of the twenty airfields in use in 1945 did not survive post-war. Shawbury Tern Hill and Cosford continue in use to this day, though Tern Hill's accommodation was turned over to the Army. High Ercall continued in use but closed in 1962, and Sleap had a new life as Shropshire's general aviation airfield. Perhaps the most obscure survivor, RAF Chetwynd, with its neat acres of grass almost lost down country lanes, is still used by the helicopters from Shawbury.

The one pre-war civilian airfield on the Long Mynd closed during the war, but reopened afterwards and thrives today. Other unlicenced private airfields operate at Shifnal, Knockin, Milson, Market Drayton and elsewhere. There is, thus, a lot of flying to be seen in the county. However, with runways often taken up, only a few small industrial estates in out of the way places, located on the old technical sites, the odd farm building of a military style, and those silent control towers remind us of days when thousands of young men and women learned the skills of aerial warfare in Shropshire.

Atcham

Shropshire's Fighter Base

RAF Atcham was built as a standard fighter base for two squadrons with a satellite at Condover. It opened in September 1941, with No. 131 being the first Spitfire squadron to move in. During June 1942 it was handed over to the United States Army Air Force as a fighter training base. American fighters proved unsuitable for European conditions, and the 309th Squadron of the 31st Fighter Group, to be based at Atcham, received thirty-five Spitfire Vs from Britain; flying began in June 1942. Here a RAF liaison officer poses with his US counterpart leaning on a Spitfire prop. The Squadron began operations during the Dieppe Raid. The former technical site is now Atcham Industrial Estate and the layout shown here on the entrance board largely follows that of the wartime buildings, hardly any of which survive.

Lightnings Arrive

The Spitfires moved south in August and were replaced by the Lockheed Lightnings of the 14th Fighter Group, who flew their aircraft from California. An RAF officer greets one of the pilots. After a period of training, not least getting used to British weather conditions, the 14th Fighter Group also moved south. The adjacent Wrekin represented a considerable flying hazard, shown here beyond the former runways. The base erected a warning beacon on the top, which could be switched on and off from Atcham control tower. After the war this task passed to High Ercall, and now resides with Shawbury.

P-47 Thunderbolts Arrive

After a period with little flying Atcham became a Combat Crew Replacement Centre equipped with P-47 Thunderbolts with up to fifty in use at any one time. Newly arrived fighter pilots, trained in the sunny skies of America, were taught about British weather and techniques. Here several are being serviced on a dispersal in front of one of the eight blister hangars at Atcham. The grave of Sgt Pilot L. G. R. Donaldson, Royal New Zealand Air Force, who died in 1942, aged twenty-three, lies in St Eata's Churchyard on the banks of the Severn, in Atcham village. Behind lie the graves of young men from Australia and Canada, a scene repeated in churchyards across Shropshire and a reminder that even training could be a dangerous business.

Atcham's Control Tower

The rear of Atcham's control tower, an expression brought to Great Britain by the Americans, replacing watch office. The white painted rocks around the paths were not just the result of military 'bull' but helped people find their way on a blacked-out field. Atcham had three large Calendar-Hamilton hangars – easily erected steel structures with corrugated iron covering. The premises of PowellGee represents the shadow of one of these, reclad and rebuilt.

Atcham's HQ Building

The stars and stripes flies at half-mast over the headquarters building, suggesting a recent accident. With a crowded flying programme (9,208 flying hours in June 1944 alone) accidents were inevitable, and there were 167 recorded accidents resulting in thirty-five fatalities. An Indian motorcycle stands outside. The surviving entrance road ran between the HQ and the motor transport workshops, which lay the other side of the adjacent lane, is still there.

Motor Transport Workshops
Trucks and jeeps stand near the MT workshops, which still exist today, though the space between them has been filled in with another building by the local farmer.

RAF Bridgnorth

Bridgnorth's Entrance

The No. 4 School of Recruit Training was opened at Stanmore in November 1939. Aircraft gate guardians did not appear until much later, and in the case of this De Havilland Vampire F3 VT801, not until the 1950s, when it had a Hurricane as a companion on the other side of the gate. The station entrance was next to the Stanmore Road. The station was not called RAF Stanmore because there was already an RAF Stanmore in Middlesex. This Vampire has since been scrapped. The entrance to Stanmore Industrial Estate is much further in, with the entrance road passing through the site of the old headquarters huts.

Recruits' Memorial

Every one of the thousands of recruits who did their basic training at Bridgnorth will have had one of these photographs of the men/boys who shared their hut. A bond built up between them, stemming from the shared trials and tribulations of drill and the other tortures of basic training, which knocked raw civilians into something resembling a military unit. The memorial to all those who served at RAF Bridgnorth, which was created on the surviving No. 3 Wing cookhouse chimney, is sited within Stanmore Country Park just to the right of the entrance road to the industrial estate.

Stanmore Country Park

Recruits were arranged into Flights for their training, and every man will have received one of these photographs upon their passing out parade. The end of national service stopped the flood of recruits to Bridgnorth and resulted in its closure in February 1963. All the wooden huts, which lay between the main technical buildings and the road, were cleared away and the site became Stanmore Country Park. This road is one that survives as the footway between the old married quarters, known as The Hobbins, and the entrance road to the industrial estate. Hickman Contractors tried to get planning permission to build a whole village in this area, with shops, pub, community centre and garage, but failed, leaving the residents of The Hobbins somewhat isolated.

Passing Out Parade

On completion of their basic training recruits took part in a passing out parade, this one clearly in the winter as they are well wrapped up in their greatcoats. Parents and siblings could come and admire the changes that had been wrought to the callow youths, who had left home such a short time before. One of the units on the industrial estate is occupied by Classic Motor Cars, who fettle classic cars, Jaguars in particular, back into showroom shape.

Spitfire

Spitfire Vb BM597 gracing the camp in the late 1950s. It had served with No. 315 and No. 317 (Polish) Squadrons during the war. This airframe was used to create the mould for the plastic Spitfires used in the film *The Battle of Britain*, which were largely destroyed in crash scenes. Restored to flight at Duxford in 1997, it is still based there but has made an emotional trip to Poland where it was met by some of its former pilots. How ironic that this BMW 328 roadster should be one of the cars restored and offered for sale by Classic Motor Cars, only yards from where the Spitfire used to be displayed.

Hawker Hunter

Hawker Hunter F5 WP191 in front of the five bay main store and gymnasium building in the centre of the camp. The Mark V was an Armstrong-Siddeley Sapphire powered aircraft. This aircraft has since been scrapped. The main store had now been refurbished, is used by Coram Showers, and lies just inside the industrial estate gates to the left.

RAF Cosford

No. 2 School of Technical Training

In 1935 the expansion of the RAF led to plans for a second School of Technical Training, after No. 1 at Halton. It was built either side of the Birmingham to Shrewsbury railway line at Cosford. These are the technical buildings and accommodation to the east of the railway line. The airfield and hangars lay on the other side. The iconic Fulton accommodation block is in the foreground with four large workshop buildings to the right. There are still a host of wooden huts, though this photo was taken in the 1970s. Like so many airfields in Shropshire, RAF Cosford has a backdrop of the Wrekin, seen here behind the hangar of the Midland Air Ambulance, an important resident of the airfield, and one of the few to actually own its own helicopter – the Airbus EC135Te G-RMAA – rather than leasing it.

Camouflaged Hangars

The Wolverhampton company of Alfred MacAlpine was contracted to build RAF Cosford – their first large contract. The contract included several E Type concrete storage hangars, designed to be covered with turf and to leave no tell-tale shadow. They were to be used by No. 9 MU for aircraft storage, and all lay on the opposite side of the airfield from the control tower and instructional hangars. The hangars are still in use, and, in a mature landscape, have a subdued impact on the scenery, unlike the Cold War building for the RAF Museum.

Instructional Hangars

On the other side of the airfield from the Type E hangars, a curved row of Type D hangars were built for instructional purposes and as further storage for No. 9 MU. Note the rail mounted crane, or 'navvy' as it was usually termed, in use by MacAlpine. One of these hangars forms a backdrop for a line of Gulf War veterans in the 2019 air show. A Tornado, Buccaneer and Jaguar are on show, all in desert pink – three instructional airframes. Recently retired aircraft served this purpose from the very opening of No. 2 School of TT.

Married Quarters
Houses under construction by MacAlpine in 1939 alongside the Newport Road for use as married quarters, with a sports stadium alongside. Eighty years later and the housing is now a mature estate.

No. 9 Maintenance Unit

In 1943, one of the major tasks undertaken by No. 9 MU was the assembly of Horsa gliders. These were built by a consortium of woodworking companies. Boulton & Paul Ltd, the former parent of the local aircraft manufacturer, built Horsa cockpits in a subsidiary in Melton Mowbray. The Horsa was probably the most wooden aircraft ever built. In 2019 the RAF Museum displays this VC10 with tail art celebrating fifty years of the aircraft's service and ninety-five years of No. 101 Squadron, which operated it. No. 101 has a long connection with Boulton Paul Aircraft, which built the FE2bs with which No. 101 was formed in 1917; the Sidestrand and Overstrand bombers, with which it was equipped in the '20s and '30s; the gun turrets on its wartime Halifax's; and the power control units on the VC10.

Secret Lancaster Bomber

In 1945/6 Boulton Paul was developing a new defensive system for the Lincoln bomber, with remotely controlled twin 20 mm cannon barbettes in dorsal and ventral positions. They used this Lancaster LL780/G to test the system, operating from Cosford (the 'G' in the serial indicates that the aircraft should be guarded at all times). It stands near the Bellman hangars by the airfield entrance. In the 2019 air show a large part of the RAF's training aircraft were lined up together: Hawks, Tucanos and Airbus H135 helicopters.

Scrapping Spitfires

In 1955 large numbers of late model Spitfires were scrapped on the far side of the airfield. This is Mk 24 PK627 awaits its fate, available for the price of its aluminium. Only a dozen years before this, the Bellman hangars on the opposite side had been a Spitfire assembly unit for the factory at Castle Bromwich. At the 2019 air show Spitfire PR XIX, on show outside the RAF Museum, draws admirers. A Spitfire's worth had grown from around £200 to £2 million.

Parade Ground ornament

For many years this Spitfire FRXIVE MT847 'flew' from a pole alongside the parade ground. Eventually it made its way inside the museum and was replaced by a Vampire T11. The Spitfire was eventually traded and is now on display at the Pima Country Aircraft Museum just outside Tucson, Arizona. The Vampire was replaced alongside the parade ground by this Hunter F6A XG225, but it later migrated to a spot alongside the museum entrance, wearing 237 OCU colours. The large welcoming banner on the side of the hangar opposite features a rendition of four examples of this same aircraft flying in formation.

Battle of Britain Open Day

The annual Cosford Air Show used to be termed a Battle of Britain Open Day. Instructional aircraft were towed out of the hangars for the day, including this Canberra B2 in 1965. Outside the same hangar in 2019 there were two Harriers, including a Sea Harrier of the Fleet Air Arm School of Flight Deck Operations, newly important with the commissioning of the Navy's new carriers.

Gliding at Cosford
The most common aircraft in the skies over Cosford used to be the gliders of the Air Training Corps and the Wrekin Gliding Club. These await a winch launch *c.* 1960. The University of Birmingham Air Squadron has long been a resident at Cosford. The current equipment is the Babcock Aerospace-owned Grob Tutor T1. G-BYVX is on display at the 2019 air show.

RAF Cosford Hospital

Cosford's 503-bed hospital opened in 1940, with a burns unit following in 1941, and treated 42,000 casualties during the Second World War. Housed in wooden buildings on the other side of the A41, away from the rest of the station, it opened to the local population after the war (including myself on one occasion – only a sprained ankle – thanks for asking.) In 1977 the hospital was closed and the buildings demolished, as shown here. New married housing now fills this site.

The National Indoor Arena

For a long while the name Cosford was best known throughout the world because, in one of the four large workshop buildings, it housed Britain's only indoor athletics arena. Here the world-record-breaking Russian pole vaulter, Sergei Bubka, attempts a clearance, and must have got uncomfortably near the roof. The large mural was painted by an inmate of Featherstone Prison, and was put on hold for a while when he escaped! On a sunny day after a very cold night the Lockheed Neptune, outside the RAF Museum, presents a postcard image.

RAF High Ercall

Post-war Aerial View
High Ercall was a large, well-dispersed airfield, befitting its primary occupant No. 29 MU. After the war large numbers of aircraft were gathered there for disposal, and in this post-war aerial view over 100 can be counted. It is said that at one point there were 1,500 awaiting scrap, many in surrounding fields. The main airfield entrance is to the right. From aircraft to cars, the main gate, still much as it was, is now the entrance to the Greenhous Fleet Operations Centre, where up to 6,000 cars are stored. The main technical site was the Road Transport Training Centre for a while.

Beaufighter Night Fighter

High Ercall was a night fighter base and on 23 April 1941 No. 68 Squadron moved in with its radar-equipped Bristol Beaufighters. This one is X7842, named *Birmingham Civil Defence*, having been paid for by the city's ARP. Two pilots and two observers are posing. No. 68 remained until May 1942. With a number of victories to their credit they moved to Coltishall and were replaced by No. 255 Squadron. High Ercall featured eight Type L hangars, which, unlike the similarly shaped Type E hangars at Cosford, were made of steel rather than concrete. They are still in use for storage, but have had the turf removed from them. These two are on No. 4 Site.

No. 1456 Flight

High Ercall was part of a novel experiment in night fighting techniques. Douglas Havoc twin engine fighters had a large Turbinlite searchlight fitted to their nose, and flew in concert with one or more Hawker Hurricanes, the idea being that the Havoc would illuminate a German raider so the Hurricanes could move in to shoot it down. At High Ercall No. 1456 Flight operated the system but it did not prove a success. Aircrew are posing in front of a Havoc, outside a Type K hangar. Still to be seen outside one of the Type K hangars on No. 2 Sub Site is this airfield defence pillbox.

Turbinlite Aircraft

This photograph has always been attributed to Tern Hill, but shows 1456 Flight Turbinlite aircraft. In the foreground is a Handley Page Harrow transport 'Boadicea', sometimes called a 'Sparrow' without the front turret. Behind is an Airspeed Oxford of No. 286 Army Co-operation Squadron, a Havoc and two black Hurricanes of 1456 Flight. The Pontoon and Dock Company, currently make Marina equipment in this Type K hangar on No. 2 Sub Site. High Ercall has a total of three Type K hangars.

Mosquito OTU

No. 60 OTU, equipped with Mosquito night fighters, operated from High Ercall late in the war. Here the crew of Flying Officer Dennis Moore (left) and his pilot, Flying Officer John Ayre, are seen in front of their Mosquito in September 1944. They went on to complete twenty-six operations together. Type J and Type K hangars flank the water tower on the main technical site at High Ercall, now used by Greenhous as the headquarters of their 35 acre Fleet Operations Centre.

Doris the Dominie

The aircraft stored by No. 29 MU at High Ercall were delivered by No. 3 Aircraft Delivery Flight, which had this De Havilland Dominie aircraft as a taxi for returning pilots to base. Originally christened *Hoof Hearted*, objections by the base commander lead to it being renamed *Doris*. The pilot is WO Sid Walker (wearing a trilby), an ex-No. 456 Defiant pilot on six-month posting in 1943. The old RAF gatehouse to No. 4 Sub Site is now in use as an office.

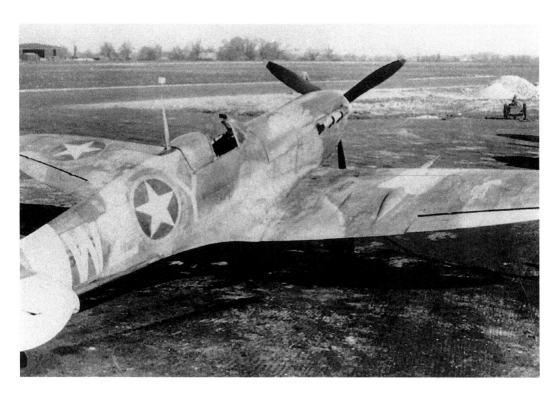

American Spitfire

When American fighter squadrons arrived in England they received Spitfires from the RAF as their own Airacobras and Lightnings were not suitable for the European theatre. This is a Mark Vb of No. 309 Squadron 31st Fighter Group at High Ercall in the summer of 1942. They left for the Mediterranean in September to become part of the Twelfth Air Force. Another Spitfire at High Ercall in 1998, but this is a full-scale fibre-glass model, albeit with original cockpit fittings, owned by Keith Jones of Cannock. It was part of the Warplane Aircraft Recovery Group Museum on No. 2 Sub Site, erected for an open day.

Aircraft Museum at High Ercall

For a short while the gatehouse to No. 2 Sub Site housed an aircraft museum, set up by the Warplane Aircraft Recovery Group, who investigated aircraft crash sites, particularly in Shropshire. The museum has since moved to Sleap. The gatehouse and adjacent building have yet to find another use. They are the nearest airfield buildings to High Ercall village.

Hinstock

Bleriot Monoplane at Hinstock

Gustav Hamel's Bleriot Monoplane, in the grounds of Hinstock Hall, at Hinstock Show on 18 July 1912. It was common for such shows to employ itinerant aviators as an extra attraction and any large field would serve as a landing place. The No. 3 on the tail was Hamel's number in the air races he regularly took part in at Hendon airfield. He had been born in Germany but was naturalised British, and was the son of the surgeon to King Edward VII. He went missing over the Channel on 23 May 1914 collecting a Morane-Saulnier Monoplane from France. Hinstock Hall during the Second World War, where officers from RAF Hinstock were billeted. It was nowhere near to the wartime airfield, which was originally named Ollerton, after the nearest village, and was in fact a lot nearer to Child's Ercall than Hinstock. That village gave its name to another airfield, which was then renamed Peplow. The two airfields were only a mile apart.

Sailors in Shropshire

Built as an SLG, Hinstock was handed over to the Fleet Air Arm, who needed a central airfield for Beam Landing Training. They named it HMS Godwit, after a wading bird. The unit was equipped with Tiger Moths and Airspeed Oxfords like the one behind this group of sailor mechanics, which includes WRENs. Most of the buildings still survive, including this toilet block on a local farm, but the airfield is hard to find down country lanes. The runways have gone being only metal tracking.

Naval Pentad Hangar
A Stinson Reliant communications aircraft outside a distinctive Pentad hangar, used largely by the Fleet Air Arm. The canted sides were convenient for housing aircraft with folding wings, though no such aircraft served at Hinstock. The same Pentad hangar is now part of the small industrial estate. It is ironically named Ollerton Business Park, using the airfield's original name, which has taken over the main technical complex and is occupied by Universal Consumer Products Plc.

Airspeed Oxford and Maintenance Crew

An Airspeed Oxford, the aircraft most widely seen in Shropshire, in front of another hangar as a backdrop of a group photograph of the maintenance staff. Near the end of the war the unit moved just down the road to the much bigger Peplow, which had been vacated by the RAF. Another Pentad hangar at Hinstock has been reclad and refurbished for use by Leyfos Plastics Ltd.

A Ship's Company

Some of the naval staff who served at Hinstock, gathered for a group photograph. Like so many others in the county, the rare naval four-storey control tower at Hinstock was derelict for many years, but was given a massive makeover, worthy of the TV show *Grand Designs*, and turned into a luxurious house.

Naval Officers

As well as Airspeed Oxfords, HMS Godwit also had a number of Tiger Moths; pilot and instructor are putting on their parachutes alongside one. Strangely, Hinstock was the only Shropshire airfield where Tiger Moths were based, whereas over the border in Staffordshire there were several. A surviving line of three Handcraft huts, which were asbestos-clad seven-sided huts bolted together. These, unusually, are raised on low brick walls.

Long Mynd

Falcons Over the Shropshire Hills

The Midland Gliding Club moved from their original base in Handsworth to the top of the Long Mynd in the 1930s. The attraction was the lift generated off the hill when a west wind blew, which made prolonged flights easier than on a flat site. Here a Slingsby Falcon glider flies high above the site in June 1936. Since then sheep and gliders have happily co-existed on the Mynd, and here a Scheibe SF25C Falke (Falcon) self-launching glider (one with a small engine), owned by the club, taxis to the end of the runway. This glider was formerly D-KGAO. The sheep seem to have learned not to lie down on the runway.

Bungee Launching

When a west wind blows on the Mynd at over 25 knots, gliders can be launched by bungee, as six sturdy club members at the end of a 'Y' shaped elastic rope trot down the hill. When it's taut the glider is catapulted into the air, flying hundreds of feet over the valley in seconds. The faithful members then walk back up the hill dragging the bungee with them, which I can testify soon becomes a tiresome process. Winch launching is the alternative when the wind is from the north or south, and this single-seat Schleicher ASK-23B is parked into the wind, awaiting its turn.

Solitary Hangar

For many years the sole building on the Mynd was the combined hangar and clubhouse in which gliders were packed, dismantled, and then erected outside. The hangar still remains and houses club gliders like this PZL SZD-31-1 G-CFZP, but most privately owned gliders are stowed away in trailers.

Winch Launching

The Midland Gliding Club pioneered a dual winch launching system, where once a glider has been launched using a large winch, the cable is returned using a second smaller winch at the other end of the field. Here gliders await their turn for launch in 1969, with a Schleicher K-13 trainer at the front of the queue. With the background of an angry sky, gliders are waiting at the opposite end of the field for winch launch, as a Schempp-Hirth Nimbus-2B G-EEFT is erected outside one of the long line of glider trailers.

RAF Peplow

Hurricane Fighter

A Hurricane fighter at Peplow, used by No. 83 OTU for fighter affiliation (where Wellington gunners practice tracking an attacking fighter). Most bomber OTUs had a handful of war-weary fighters attached to them for this purpose. The solitary T2 hangar still in use (four were originally on site) next to the road between Eaton-upon-Tern and Child's Ercall, which follows the line of the airfield perimeter road.

Aerial Photograph
An aerial photograph of Peplow being rebuilt in 1942. It had been an all-grass SLG for Tern Hill and then Shawbury, but was enlarged as a Wellington bomber OTU. Strangely all three runways intersect, which would have put them all out of action after one crash at the intersection. The AML Bombing Teacher building, in which wartime bomb aimers were trained by peering through a bomb sight in an elevated position over a moving map. It is slowly being refurbished, presumably as an unusual house.

Horsa Glider Training

In 1944 the Wellington bombers moved out. Peplow was one of several Shropshire airfields used to train Horsa glider pilots and their aircraft tugs in preparation for the invasion of Europe. This is the cockpit of a Horsa glider at the de Havilland Aircraft Museum. The Horsa was the most wooden aircraft ever built – even the control wheels were wood. A Horsa returned to Shropshire in the 1990s when the Assault Glider Trust built this exact replica at RAF Shawbury. It moved to Cosford for storage in 2014, but could find no permanent home in the county, and was shipped to Arnhem in Holland in June 2019.

A Piece of Cake

For a while a number of private light aircraft were kept in a small hangar at Peplow, using a section of the perimeter track as a runway. They included this Saab Safir, owned by Dave Williams, a local garage owner, who decided to fly it under the bridge that had just been completed on the Hinstock bypass. The road was not yet open, I hasten to add. With mature trees and large trucks appearing round the bend on the road these days, it's hard to imagine the feat being repeated. In actual fact it's hard to believe he did it in the first place.

RAF Rednal

Shropshire's Spitfire Base

RAF Rednal opened in April 1942 with a satellite at Montford Bridge and as the home for the Spitfires of No. 61 OTU. From there to the end of the war Spitfires filled the skies of western Shropshire, including this one which sits at a dispersal, trolley-ack attached, ready for start-up. It also has a fuel bowser alongside. It still bears the codes of No. 52 OTU. An aircraft still graces Rednal at the gate of the paintballing centre in front of the derelict control tower, ex-Royal Navy Westland Wessex XT480.

Spitfire Accidents

RAF personnel examine a Spitfire with a collapsed undercarriage at Rednal, though this one has the 'TO' codes more usually worn by No. 61 OTU's Masters, Martinets and Harvards. The derelict control tower is now draped with netting associated with the paintballing centre.

Famous French Ace Pierre Clostermann

One of the most famous pilots to be trained at Rednal was the top-scoring French fighter pilot Pierre Closterman, with thirty-three victories to his credit. Trained as a commercial pilot in California, he came to England and was trained at Rednal, which he mentioned in less than glowing terms in his post-war bestselling book *The Big Show*. This is a Spitfire at dispersal at Rednal. The gatehouse to Site B at Rednal is now the home of a sign-making company. Rednal Industrial Estate is split into two main sites in the former technical buildings.

Dakota Casualty Evacuation
A row of ten Dakotas and several ambulances are lined up at Rednal. In the immediate aftermath of D-Day around 1,750 casualties were airlifted to Rednal to be taken to local hospitals. Many of the Maycrete wartime buildings are in use in externally unrestored form. As they were only expected to have a working life of half a dozen years, they are doing reasonably well over seventy-five years on.

Film Making at Rednal

During the war a film was planned about the air-fighting in the Greek campaign; it was to be called *Signed with their Honour* or *The Air War in Greece*. Several Gloster Gladiators were gathered at Rednal for the flying sequences. Shooting began, but was cancelled after a couple of accidents. Presumably Spitfires like this one would have to be carefully placed out of shot during the filming, as there were no Spitfires in Greece. The large dining hall on Site B still survives, though is currently without a tenant.

Spitfire Take-off
Two student pilots stroll back from their Spitfires after a flight. Contests of a different nature are now possible at Rednal, as the junction of two runways features Rednal Karting's racecourse.

RAF Shawbury

First World War Trainers

An airfield for flight training was constructed at Shawbury during the First World War, and one of the types in use was the De Havilland DH6, which was designed as the simplest and cheapest training aircraft to build, operate and repair. It is seen on a snowy day probably in the winter of 1917–18. The airfield closed after the war but was reopened and rebuilt on twice the scale for the Second World War, the entrance being just outside Shawbury village, on the eatsern side. The technical buildings were on the western side in the First World War.

Avro 504K Crash
The ubiquitous Avro 504K was also used at Shawbury. Here 952 has crashed on one of the surrounding lanes. No. 27 MU and No. 11 Service Fling Training School occupied Shawbury during the war and had four of these Type L Aircraft Storage hangars. This one is on Site E, now occupied by a riding school.

The Aries Flights

The Lancaster *Aries* at Shawbury, from where it took off for the first round the world flight by a British aircraft in October 1944. It was part of a series of long distance navigation exercises that were later to include flights over the North Pole. The aircraft later had its camouflage paint and the gun turrets removed and a streamlined nose fitted. A view across Shawbury today shows the same Type C hangar that was behind the *Aries* and the new post-war control tower to the right.

Flight Training at Shawbury
Three Chipmunks of the ATC Air Experience Flight. WG362 was later scrapped but the cockpit is now with No. 2523 ATC Squadron, Linton, Cambridgeshire. WZ877 is still flying, privately owned in La Rochelle, France. The two most famous pupils of the current Defence Helicopter Training School, Prince William and Prince Harry, here with their instructors in front of one of the school's Bell Griffin helicopters.

Javelin Scrapping
During the late 1960s and early 1970s large numbers of Gloster Javelins were scrapped at Shawbury, and seven aircraft can be counted here on the Site D area. An Airbus Juno HT1 ZM524 from the Defence Helicopter Training School at Shawbury, on display at RAF Cosford for the 2019 air show.

Aircraft Scrapping Area

Around 1970 it was possible to walk through the wood on the north-west corner of Shawbury and out into a large aircraft scrapping area, with a variety of types scattered about undergoing the chop, like this Twin Pioneer, standing just behind a Shackleton. This same area has now been returned to farmland, though a tall radar tower occupies the space where the Twin-Pin stood.

Training Jets

A Gloster Meteor T7 WF787 awaits the scrap man on Site A – another just behind. Some years later another Meteor T7 WF791 was actually operated from Shawbury, along with a De Havilland Vampire T11 XH304, as the Central Flying School's Vintage Pair. Vampires had served at Shawbury with the School of Air Traffic Control. Tragically they collided and crashed during a display at Mildenhall in 1986.

Blackburn Beverley Graveyard

In the late 1960s a number of Blackburn Beverleys were scrapped at Shawbury, many, like this one, with Middle Eastern camouflage. In 1969 I climbed the ladder to the cockpit of one and found a map still on the navigator's table marked with an up-country flight in Aden, its last operational sortie before being returning home. Today this is a surviving Type D hangar on Site A. Shawbury was blessed with a surprising variety of hangar types spread over a huge area, though many have been demolished over recent years.

RAF Sleap

RAF Sleap was built as a satellite for RAF Tilstock and the Whitleys of No. 81 OTU, but it did not open until 15 January 1943, when C Flight arrived. There were numerous flying accidents, including this overshoot, though the most serious occurred at 3.00 a.m. on 27 August, and 12.20 p.m. on 8 September 1943, when a Whitley veered off the runway and crashed into the control tower. In the first accident, which was on landing, nine people were injured – three in the tower. In the second, on take-off, seven people were killed including three in the tower, two of them WAAFs. The control tower today shows little sign of the crashes, which involved fierce fires, and it watches over the only licenced general aviation airfield in Shropshire.

Control Caravan

During the 1950s Sleap became a satellite of Shawbury and the Central Navigation and Control School, training air traffic controllers, and the runways were refurbished. This Ground Control Caravan was sited there, and trainees controlled landings by Vampire T11s and Provosts. A sign of changing times in the twenty-first century was the basing of several Russian aircraft at Sleap, including this Yak-52 aerobatic aircraft, shown taxiing by the control tower.

The Arrival of Private Aircraft

In 1955 the Shropshire Aero Club was formed and based at Sleap, though the runways were still used by the RAF. The club was based in a building on the far side of the airfield, next to the sole surviving blister hangar. This 1945-built Miles Messenger 4B G-AKVZ is shown to the rear of the control tower. The aircraft was still flying in 2016 when it suffered an accident during take-off at Biggin Hill, a ground loop following by an undercarriage collapse. In 2019 this same area is used for car parking. The wartime Handcraft hut to the right of the tower still survives, and the tower has acquired a rooftop control booth, the first floor having become a café.

Whitley on Runway

An Auster receives a wheel change during a 1960s fly-in at Sleap. Another sign of the times was when Glenn James, owned this Russian Yak 3U fighter (new build), registered in Germany as D-FYGJ. Glenn also owned a Yak11, and currently has an Avro Anson.

Whitley Overshoot by the Line to Wem

As part of the preparations for D-Day, No. 81 OTU switched to Horsa glider towing during late 1943. This Whitley suffered a massive overshoot, ending up almost on the Shrewsbury to Wem railway line, which is over a mile from the airfield. The solitary surviving blister hangar on the far side has now been joined by a whole village of assorted new hangars.

Visiting Percival Provost
During a fly-in in the 1960s, this Percival Provost, of the Central Navigation and Control School, flew in from Shawbury, where the Provost was shortly to be retired. The RAF had given up control of Sleap in 1961, but still used the runways. A Provost returned to Sleap in 2008 when the Staffordshire Aircraft Restoration Team placed WW388 on loan with the Warplane Aircraft Recovery Group Museum. It had already been displayed in museums at Long Marston, Firbeck and Hemswell, but was never to be erected at Sleap, and left untouched, a year later, going into private ownership.

RAF Tern Hill

Heavy Bombers Come to Shropshire

Tern Hill was started in 1916 as a Royal Flying Corps training station, with Avro 504 aircraft and others, but in 1918 it was decided to work up heavy bomber squadrons equipped with the new Handley Page O/400s. This one, outside one of the hangars, is fitted with Sunbeam Maori engines. The aircraft behind appears to be a single engine RE7. On the south side of the airfield this D Type hangar, formerly used by No. 24 MU, now closed, has been in use as the Maurice Chandler sports arena for some time.

The Army at Tern Hill

As the Royal Flying Corps was part of the Army, Tern Hill was actually built as an Army establishment. This is another picture of a Maori-powered Handley Page O/400, a number of which were destroyed in a post-war hangar fire. By then the Royal Air Force had been established. Things came full circle when the Army took over the accommodation units at Tern Hill, renaming them Clive Barracks, though the airfield remains in use by the RAF.

Night Fighter Crew at Tern Hill

As well as housing No. 5 Flying Training School and No. 24 MU, Tern Hill also had night fighters based to cover the North West, but this is a No. 256 Sqd. Defiant crew normally based at Squires Gate, Blackpool. The pilot, Flt Lt Christopher Deanesley, and his gunner, Sgt Jack Scott, moved forward to Tern Hill with eight other Defiants on 10 May 1941, in anticipation of a 'fighter night' over Birmingham. At 21.55 hrs they took off and just before midnight came across a Heinkel He111 over Smethwick, which Scott shot down. They landed back at Tern Hill after the first of four victories they were to claim. The entrance to the station, now Clive Barracks, was, at the time of this photograph, occupied by the Royal Irish Regiment.

Fire Dump Javelin

Most RAF stations used old aircraft for fire crew practice. This Gloster Javelin was consumed at Tern Hill in the late 1960s. Tern Hill is now the local centre for Air Training Corps flying and this Grob Vigilant T1 ZH185 is on the strength of No. 632 Volunteer Gliding School.

Percival Provost

After the war, when the Miles Master had been the most familiar sight at Tern Hill, No. 6 Service Flying Training School moved in, equipped with Percival Provosts like this one seen at an air display. When the Jet Provost initiated all-through jet training, the Tern Hill runways were too short, and fixed wing trainers left. The most common helicopter seen at Tern Hill during the 1970s and '80s were the Sud Aviation Gazelles from Shawbury. This one is on an 'away day' visiting the Weston Park Air Show in 1986.

Helicopter Training
In 1961 the Central Flying School helicopter training unit arrived at Tern Hill. This Sycamore XE320 was on its strength. The Gazelles from Shawbury were replaced by Squirrel T1s, like this one taking part in a fly-in at Halfpenny Green in 2011. Shawbury's helicopters are the most common sights in the skies of Shropshire, using not just Tern Hill and Chetwynd, but a number of fields owned by compliant farmers.

RAF Tilstock

Whitley Bombers on Whitchurch Heath
Tilstock opened on 1 August 1942 as RAF Whitchurch Heath, being renamed the following year to avoid confusion with Whitchurch near Bristol. It housed the Whitleys of No. 81 OTU with a satellite at Sleap. As the runways spread across the A41, that road was closed for the duration. A surviving B1 hangar, featuring a volleyball net, stands next to the existing parachute club on the eastern side of the A41.

A Stirling Bomber Ends Up on the A49

The Whitleys were concentrated on Sleap for glider towing training from 1944. Tilstock housed No. 1665 Heavy Bomber Conversion Unit with up to fifty Short Stirlings on strength. This one overshot the runway and ended up on the A49. Flying continues at Tilstock on a short section of runway on the eastern side, with Skydive Tilstock Freefall Club's aircraft housed in this small hangar. The club has been at Tilstock since 1964 – the longest serving parachuting site in the UK.

Runway Signaller
A signaller controlling aircraft movements in a Ground Control Caravan alongside one of Tilstock's runways. The woods to the south of the airfield are well known for containing many derelict former wartime buildings including several Romney huts like this one.

Tilstock Control Tower

A rare visitor (in 1952) to Tilstock was this Army Air Corps Auster AOP6 VW993, on an exercise. The squaddies in attendance do not look like they are enjoying the very wet weather. Recently an imaginative restoration of the control tower has been funded by the Lottery and Nature England and Butterfly Conservation, with sign boards recording the history of Whitchurch Heath.

Other Airfields

RAF Bratton

Seven naval aviators relax on the side of an air-raid shelter at the Satellite Landing Ground at Bratton, just north of Wellington. Attached to HMS Godwit, Hinstock for some time, Bratton also acted as an SLG for Shawbury and Tern Hill, but was never more than a small grass airfield with just five blister hangars. The buildings in the top picture can still be seen today within what is a tiny industrial estate just off the A442.

Airspeed Oxford

The aircraft most often seen at Bratton was the Airspeed Oxford trainer, like this one, belonging to the Beam Landing School at Hinstock, though the Oxfords from Shawbury were a more familiar sight. A view of the Wrekin across the airfield, now farmers' fields, from the small technical area. The Wrekin is a backdrop to so many of Shropshire's airfields.

RAF Brockton

Near to Sutton Maddock, RAF Brockton was a Relief Landing Ground for No. 9 MU at Cosford, where aircraft were stored. This is a picture of the entire staff, who were mostly civilians. Shropshire's first aircraft landing was here on 31 July 1911 when James Valentine arrived in his Deperdussin Monoplane. A single Robin hangar still survives in use today, down a track behind the Mason's Arms in Kemberton. The airfield's watch office and canteen have been incorporated into a private bungalow.

RAF Chetwynd

Probably the quietest and most minimal RAF airfield in the country is RAF Chetwynd, a small grass field down country lanes north of Newport. Opened in 1941 as an SLG for RAF Tern Hill's Miles Masters, it is still in use today for the helicopters from Shawbury. A small two-storey Portakabin was erected next to the wartime building as a largely unmanned watch office. Today a slightly larger Portakabin serves the same function, with a new radio tower behind. Very occasionally Hercules aircraft are said to land at night, undertaking clandestine exercises.

RAF Condover

Built as a satellite for the Spitfire fighter base at Atcham, a Spitfire coming in to land like this one at Rednal turned out to be a rare sight. Atcham was assigned to the Americans and Condover became a satellite for RAF Shawbury. The derelict control tower is one of a number of buildings that still survive at Condover, including the floodlight trailer and tractor shed behind.

Airspeed Oxfords Arrive

The Airspeed Oxford was the aircraft most associated with Condover, when it became a satellite of RAF Shawbury, especially when Shawbury was having its own paved runways built. Nevertheless despite being a substantial three-runway airfield, Condover was underused. A re-clad T1 hangar survives in the technical area, which has become a small industrial estate on the other side of the lane between the villages of Condover and Frodesley.

Local Fighter Ace Eric Lock

The top-scoring British-born fighter pilot of the Battle of Britain, Eric Lock, was born at Bomere on the lane between Condover and Bayston Hill. He worked on his father's Bomere Farm, moving to Allfield Farm in 1933, even nearer to Condover, and also worked at the family quarry in Sharpstones Lane (now a huge hole in the ground). He joined the RAFVR before the war and, after being called up, came home to marry Peggy Meyers – an ex-Miss Shrewsbury – at St Julien's Church in July 1940. His short stature gave him the nickname 'sawn-off'. The current industrial estate at the site of RAF Condover's technical area would still have been a farmer's field if Eric and his new bride chose to stroll by just after their marriage before his return to No. 41 Squadron.

Flt Lt Eric Lock DSO, DFC (and Bar)
Eric Lock had sixteen victories during the Battle of Britain, and is shown in his No. 611 Squadron Spitfire with his final total of twenty-six indicated (plus nine 'probables'). Shortly before this he had flown his Spitfire low over his parents' house and the airfield under construction at Condover. He had just returned to action after recovering from injuries received during the third time he was shot down. On 3 August 1941 he went missing over the Channel. One of the wartime huts at Condover now in use in a riding school.

RAF Hodnet

The staff at RAF Hodnet in front of one of their charges, a Lockheed Hudson. Hodnet was a RLG used to store aircraft by three of the local MUs, with the landing area south of the A53 and the aircraft mostly stored north of it in the grounds of Hodnet Hall. Two small wartime buildings survive, both in use by the local cricket club as a clubhouse and mower/roller shed.

Monkmoor Aircraft Acceptance Park
The First World War training airfield at Monkmoor, Shrewsbury, was also an Aircraft Acceptance Park where new aircraft were delivered and prepared for service. There were three large double-bay hangars with Belfast Truss roofs, which can be seen in this photograph, with a Vickers Vimy bomber being worked on, *c.* 1919. One of them is in use as a carpet warehouse, which has actually removed the suspended ceiling it used to have to reveal the Belfast Truss in all its glory.

Joy Riding Comes to Monkmoor

Berkshire Aviation Services, which had been formed in 1921 as an itinerant joy riding company, used Monkmoor as a base in 1928–29, and on 15 May 1929, three of their Avro 504Ks can be seen giving joy flights to local people, including G-EBOB. The hangars can be seen in the background. Those same hangars are still in use by a number of different companies, but the airfield has been largely built upon.

Five Shillings a Flight

Flights were typically five shillings a time, little more than a solitary circuit, with two people crammed in the rear cockpit. Here a ground crew member helps them up the ladder, while the pilot keeps the engine running for a swift turnaround. This is claimed to be in 1927. One small First World War office still survives and is in use as a hair salon.

RAF Montford Bridge

Built as a satellite for No. 61 OTU at Rednal, Montford Bridge had a minimal amount of buildings – just four blister hangars and three temporary canvas-clad Bessoneaus. One of the pilots trained at Montford Bridge was Raymond Baxter, later to become a famous BBC broadcaster. During his six months at Montford Bridge he went to a party at Atcham and met his future wife, Sylvia Kathryn Johnson, an American nurse. Here his 602 Squadron Spitfire carries her name Sylvia K.

The control tower, or watch office, at Montford Bridge originally consisted of the single-storey section to the right, the two-storey part being added later for a better view. It stands derelict in a farmer's field.

The Big Show

France's top-scoring fighter pilot of the war, with thirty-three victories, was Pierre Closterman who later wrote his bestseller about his experiences, *The Big Show*. He learned to fly commercially in California, but travelled to Great Britain in 1942 and joined the RAF. He was trained on Spitfires at No. 61 OTU Rednal and Montford Bridge. One of the buildings at Montford Bridge now serves as a stable. A small number of buildings survive including this Maycrete hut, and remains of the runways can still be seen.

RAF Weston Park

No. 9 MU at RAF Cosford had a RLG at nearby Weston Park. The runway lay alongside the Offoxey Road, and the aircraft were stored in the grounds of stately home Weston Park, the home of the Earl of Bradford, a section of wall being demolished to tow them through. Strangely the aircraft were stored across the boundary in Staffordshire, but the runway was in Shropshire. The derelict tractor shed and office lay by the road for many years. Eventually it was incorporated into a new bungalow. Who would think there was ever an airfield here, so true of many of the airfields of Shropshire.

Acknowledgements

A host of lovely people have given me photographs of Shropshire airfields over the years, and I have to thank Toby Neal of the *Shropshire Star*, in particular, for introducing me to some of them. Others to whom I owe thanks include Barry Abraham, David Adams, Peter Broom, Wing Cdr Christopher Deanesley, Ron Howard, Les Jones, Sqn Ldr Martin Locke, Sir Alfred MacAlpine & Son Ltd, Vaughan Meers, Major Ervin Miller, Gary Pearson, George Preece, Brian Robinson, Keith Seddon, Andy Simpson, Skydive Tilstock, R. C. Sturtivant, Andy Thomas, Flt Sgt Sid Walker, Dave Welch and Dave Williams. I have not always been efficient at keeping track of which person lent which photograph, so if I have missed your name, please forgive me.